MAY 2017

The Cute Boot

Jan Westberg

Consulting Editor, Diane Craig, M.A./Reading Specialist

ABDO
Publishing Company

Published by ABDO Publishing Company, 4940 Viking Drive, Edina, Minnesota 55435.

Credits
Edited by: Pam Price
Curriculum Coordinator: Nancy Tuminelly
Cover and Interior Design and Production: Mighty Media
Photo and Illustration Credits: BananaStock Ltd., Brand X Pictures, Comstock, Creatas, Digital Vision, Eyewire Images, Hemera, ImageState, PhotoDisc, Stockbyte, Jan Westberg

Library of Congress Cataloging-in-Publication Data

Westberg, Jan.
      The cute boot / Jan Westberg.
         p. cm. -- (Rhyme time)
      Includes index.
      ISBN 1-59197-783-5
      1. English language--Rhyme--Juvenile literature. I. Title. II. Rhyme time (ABDO Publishing Company)

PE1517.W476 2004
428.1'3--dc22

                                                                                    2004047249

SandCastle™ books are created by a professional team of educators, reading specialists, and content developers around five essential components that include phonemic awareness, phonics, vocabulary, text comprehension, and fluency. All books are written, reviewed, and leveled for guided reading, early intervention reading, and Accelerated Reader® programs and designed for use in shared, guided, and independent reading and writing activities to support a balanced approach to literacy instruction.

Let Us Know

After reading the book, SandCastle would like you to tell us your stories about reading. What is your favorite page? Was there something hard that you needed help with? Share the ups and downs of learning to read. We want to hear from you! To get posted on the ABDO Publishing Company Web site, send us e-mail at:

sandcastle@abdopub.com

SandCastle Level: Transitional

Words that rhyme do not have to be spelled the same. These words rhyme with each other:

boot

pollute

cute

root

flute

shoot

fruit

suit

hoot

toot

Jessica's mom spun her so fast that she almost lost a boot!

Robert's new puppy is very cute.

The owl says hoot!

Kelsey likes to play the flute.

James and his friends root for their team.

Green grapes are Diana's favorite **fruit**.

Thomas thinks squirt guns are fun to shoot.

They spent the day picking up bottles and other things that **pollute** the beach.

Ann's party horn makes a loud **toot!**

Max and Spencer are each wearing a **suit**.

The Cute Boot

There once was a man
who wore one boot.

The boot he wore
was very cute.

The man with one cute boot
lived on a farm and tried to grow fruit.

He planted the seeds,
but they wouldn't take root.

The man was careful not to pollute.

He didn't understand why his fruit wouldn't take root.

HOOT!!!

The man with the cute boot
suddenly heard a hoot.

18

Up in the tree was an owl with a flute.

As the owl began to toot on the flute, the man saw his fruit start to take root.

Up came the plants, shoot after shoot.

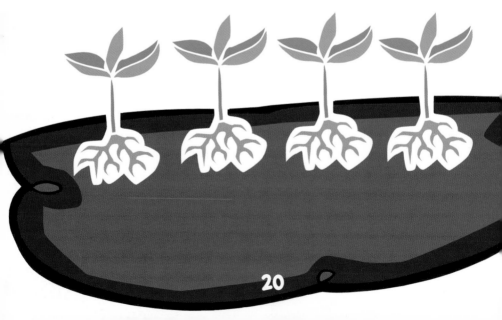

Soon there was
plenty of fruit
for the man
with one cute boot.

Rhyming Riddle

What do you call an outfit you wear when you play a wind instrument?

Flute suit

Glossary

pollute. to contaminate the air, water, or soil with manmade waste

root. to cheer

shoot. to fire a gun or water gun; new plant growth

suit. a set of matching clothes, usually a jacket with pants or a skirt

take root. a common saying that means to become established or to become rooted

About SandCastle™

A professional team of educators, reading specialists, and content developers created the SandCastle™ series to support young readers as they develop reading skills and strategies and increase their general knowledge. The SandCastle™ series has four levels that correspond to early literacy development in young children. The levels are provided to help teachers and parents select the appropriate books for young readers.

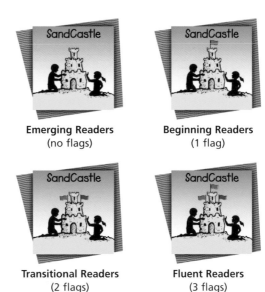

Emerging Readers
(no flags)

Beginning Readers
(1 flag)

Transitional Readers
(2 flags)

Fluent Readers
(3 flags)

These levels are meant only as a guide. All levels are subject to change.

ABDO
Publishing Company

To see a complete list of SandCastle™ books and other nonfiction titles from ABDO Publishing Company, visit www.abdopub.com or contact us at:
4940 Viking Drive, Edina, Minnesota 55435 • 1-800-800-1312 • fax: 1-952-831-1632